Illustration from a postcard entitled 'Home Sweet Home' dating from 1909.

THE EDWARDIAN HOME

YVONNE BELL

For John

Published in 2010 by Shire Publications Ltd,
Midland House, West Way, Botley, Oxford OX2 0PH.
(Website: www.shirebooks.co.uk)

Copyright © 2005 by Yvonne Bell.
First published 2005. Reprinted 2009 and 2010.
Shire Library 443. ISBN 978 0 74780 631 8.
Yvonne Bell is hereby identified as the author of this work
in accordance with Section 77 of the Copyright, Designs
and Patents Act 1988.

British Library Cataloguing in Publication Data:
Bell, Yvonne
The Edwardian home. – (Shire Library; 443)
1. Architecture, Domestic – Great Britain – History – 20th
century 2. Architecture, Edwardian – Great Britain 3.
Dwellings – Great Britain – History – 20th century 4.
House furnishings – Great Britain – History – 20th century
5. Decoration and ornament – Edwardian style 6. Great
Britain – Social life and customs – 20th century I. Title
728'.0941'09041 ISBN 0 7478 0631 4.

Cover: *A painting by Thomas Friedenson (1879–1931) from 'The Garden City' by C. B. Purdom (J. M. Dent & Sons, 1913).*

ACKNOWLEDGEMENTS

My thanks go to: Robert Lancaster, Curator of the First Garden City Heritage Museum, Letchworth; the owner of the Debenham House, Holland Park, London and Tim McDermott; Sandy Kitching, Lakeland Arts Trust (Blackwell); the National Trust (Standen, Sunnycroft); the National Trust for Scotland (The Hill House); London's Transport Museum; Jane Taylor, Heal's; Marita Medelis, Archivist – Harrods; Mr and Mrs Martin Saunders; David Beevers, Preston Manor; Tom Taylor, Folly Farm; Trevor Smith; Philip Binding; Denise Powell; and Val Seeley. Very special thanks to my husband for all the photographic work.

Illustrations are acknowledged as follows: Philip Binding, page 14 (top); the owner of the Debenham House, Holland Park, London, back cover, pages 6 (bottom left and right), 11 (bottom), 27 (bottom right), 28 (bottom right), 34 (all), 35 (bottom), 43 (top left), 45, 54 (top); First Garden City Heritage Museum, Letchworth, pages 3, 8 (bottom), 17 (top), 41 (top), 49 (top); Company Archive, Harrods Ltd, London, pages 26 (top), 32 (bottom), 38 (centre); Heal & Son Limited, page 40 (top); Lakeland Arts Trust (Blackwell), pages 5, 22 (bottom), 27 (bottom left); Cadbury Lamb, page 13; London's Transport Museum, page 7; the National Trust, Standen (NTPL Rupert Truman), page 4; the National Trust, Sunnycroft (NTPL Bill Batten), page 20 (top); the National Trust for Scotland (The Hill House), page 23 (top); Royal Pavilion, Libraries and Museums, Brighton and Hove, page 24 (bottom); Mr and Mrs Martin Saunders, pages 16 (centre), 21 (top), 27 (top), 29 (top), 30 (both), 31 (top), 35 (right), 37 (bottom); Trevor Smith, pages 15 (bottom), 16 (top). Other photographs are by the author's husband, John Bell, and other illustrations from the author's collection.

Printed in China through Worldprint Ltd

CONTENTS

'At that period of history the whole contentment of life seemed to depend on whether you had been sufficiently fortunate to get yourself born in the proper social niche, or whether you had not. Whatever niche you appeared in, save of course the top one of them all which was the aristocracy, you had to struggle to present to the outside world a representative picture which gave the impression that you were far better off than they imagined … Home was the best central stage on which you could demonstrate this.'

　　Ursula Bloom, *Sixty Years of Home* (Hurst & Blackett, 1960)

Pix Road, Letchworth Garden City, Hertfordshire.

4

Standen near East Grinstead, West Sussex, designed by Philip Webb, one of William Morris's closest friends and colleagues. The house (National Trust) grows out of the surrounding landscape: it is built of local bricks and sandstone quarried from the garden.

INTRODUCTION

The Edwardian period, from around the end of the nineteenth century to the First World War of 1914–18, is generally overlooked, sandwiched as it is between the high romance of the long Victorian era and the modernity of the 1920s and 1930s. Edward VII's reign was short (1901–10), but it was a time of enormous changes that would leave their imprint on the whole of the twentieth century. These changes were already being felt in the dying years of Victoria's reign and were to continue until the upheaval of the First World War, which brought to an end what in retrospect has often been considered something of a golden age.

Victorian Britain had been prosperous and by the turn of the new century Great Britain, as well as many private individuals, enjoyed enormous wealth. This led to a great outpouring of ostentatious consumerism that percolated through much of society. The last castle to be built in England (Castle Drogo in Devon, designed by Edwin Lutyens) was begun in 1910, while great new country houses were constructed and existing ones updated and equipped with the newest ideas and furnishings. The numerous middle classes, driven by the aspiration to move up the social ladder, longed to copy their 'betters' and took up the new ideas with enthusiasm.

Although there was still much poverty, state pensions, sickness payments and other welfare benefits began during this period and started to improve the lives of the working classes. At the same time several wealthy employers were concerned for the needs of their workers and sought to provide more suitable housing for them.

These were exciting years, with all the benefits of a highly industrialised society to enjoy. Motor cars, tractors, omnibuses and aeroplanes were all new, and factory production lines turned out everything householders felt they required for modern living. In reaction to this mechanisation a great nostalgia for the past was created – a feeling that village life was preferable to the vast industrialised conurbations, and a longing for the return of craftsmanship and individual design in houses and their contents.

From around the middle of the nineteenth century artists and writers such as Augustus Pugin, John Ruskin and William Morris, feeling that the Industrial Revolution had devalued craftsmen, urged freedom of expression and 'honesty' in design. Architects, designers and craftsmen came together in the Arts and Crafts movement, which, by the new century, had become well established.

Blackwell (1898–1900), the 'Arts and Crafts House' in Cumbria, designed by Baillie Scott. This house was built as a holiday home for a wealthy patron. The architect had freedom of design, unrestricted by domestic necessities. The house has been restored by the Lakeland Arts Trust and contains many original features; it includes furnishings and craftwork of the period.

The Debenham House (1906) in Holland Park, London, was designed by Halsey Ricardo for Ernest Debenham, the store magnate. This black and white photograph from 'Everywoman's Encyclopaedia' (about 1912) illustrated an article on 'The Dustproof House' but could not do justice to the vibrant colours of the glazed bricks and tiles used in its design.

Above: *The tilework in Debenham House, London, is an outstanding example of the craftsmanship of William de Morgan, who was a keen admirer of William Morris and one of the leading lights of the Arts and Crafts movement.*

Left: *The lily was a very fashionable flower in Edwardian times, often found on decorative tiles for fireplaces. Here it is part of a delicately inlaid Art Nouveau design in wood and mother-of-pearl, used as part of the panelling in the library of Debenham House, London.*

According to the principles of the Arts and Crafts movement, houses were to be built of local materials, with architects looking to the past for inspiration, taking the local vernacular into consideration and employing craftsmen in the construction. The Arts and Crafts houses built towards the end of the nineteenth century and during the Edwardian period, such as the Debenham House in Holland Park, London, Standen in Sussex, and Blackwell in the Lake District, are very beautiful and refreshingly innovative. Perhaps not surprisingly, they were extremely expensive to construct and could be afforded only by the very rich.

Gradually, however, industry and the Arts and Crafts movement formed links as the market-place produced a demand for some of the design ideas now becoming fashionable. With the 'tube' train, motor car, omnibus and tram making travel easy, it was possible to live further from work, shops and entertainment. New suburbs sprang up on the fringes of cities with a completely different style of living.

A 1908 poster for Golders Green Underground station. Such posters painted a rosy picture of life in the new suburbs.

This terrace of houses in Letchworth, Hertfordshire, incorporates the basic principles of grander Arts and Crafts houses with its enveloping tiled roof and simple rendering. Although built in the early part of the twentieth century, it still looks remarkably modern.

In 1903 the first Garden City was begun at Letchworth, Hertfordshire. The idea was to plant a community in the countryside where people could both live and work in harmonious surroundings. Leading Arts and Crafts architects of the time were employed in the design of the houses, whether large detached homes for the better off or terraced cottages for labourers. For reasons of economy these homes were scaled-down versions of much grander houses but they were well

Houses as above can be built on Garden City for £370.

A. COLLINS, Builder, Garden City

An advertisement for a house, priced at £370. Note the use of the description 'Artistic Appearance' – in fashionable circles 'artistic' was a favourite word.

A GOOD ADDRESS.

'A Good Address' ('Punch', November 1913). House names such as 'The Grange' gave a cachet to somewhat smaller houses. The couple are flattered to receive a catalogue for liveries for chauffeurs, grooms, footmen and other staff.

designed and included many Arts and Crafts features, and soon other such new towns and suburbs emerged.

At this time great numbers of people rented their homes and private ownership was far less common than today. While a house by the architect Baillie Scott could cost £2,300 to build, including stables and outbuildings, a billiard room, eight bedrooms and two bathrooms, a large pleasant villa with garden in Balham, south London, could cost £850. A ten-roomed house near the coast with orchard and stabling was available at an annual rental of £30; a six-roomed well-furnished cottage outside Bath could be rented for 10 shillings (50 pence) per week. A three-bedroomed country cottage could be bought for £150 and rented for 5 shillings per week, and even lower rents were paid by the poor for very inadequate housing indeed.

The spread of new ideas in housing fostered an increased interest in the home and its furnishings. The first Ideal Home Exhibition was held in 1908, sponsored by the *Daily Mail*. In the suburbs a renewed pride in their home led homeowners to give even modest houses a name – many of the 'Elms', 'Laurels', 'Holmes', 'Hursts' and 'Crofts' derive from this period.

'A Country Cottage and Garden' designed by Claud J. Kay, as illustrated in 'The Studio Magazine' of 1912, a journal that upheld the aims of the Arts and Crafts movement. The sum of £1,200 was stipulated as the limit of the cost for this house, exclusive of site, and was considered 'a fair, and even generous allowance'.

ARCHITECTURAL STYLES

The Edwardian house was subject to such a variety of influences that it is difficult to distil them all into a specific style.

The architects of the Arts and Crafts movement designed houses that seemed at one with the landscape and looked as if they had evolved naturally over the centuries. Tall brick chimneys grew out of the ground and deep roofs enveloped the house 'like a soft felt hat' – the perfect description of a Lutyens roof. Small windows were placed in seemingly random fashion in wide expanses of plain walls, often rendered or of rough stonework. Deep gables and leaded windows harked back to the Elizabethan tradition, as did oak beams and red brickwork.

The materials used in building were themselves seen as of artistic value and interest. Nowhere is this better displayed than in the design of the Debenham House (1906) in Holland Park, London, by Halsey Ricardo, one of the eminent architects involved in the Letchworth Garden City project. Here pale terracotta and coloured glazed bricks and tilework defined the lines of the house with colour rather than decorative detail. It

The deep enveloping roof, small leaded windows and plain walls of this seaside house are some of the Arts and Crafts details that remained popular throughout the twentieth century.

has remained fresh and bright, as the materials used have protected it against possible corrosion by the city atmosphere, and is considered an outstanding example of the Arts and Crafts home, combining as it does the work of so many leaders of the movement.

Halsey Ricardo's Debenham House, 1906. Sir John Betjeman called it 'the most beautiful Edwardian house in London'. Here the green tiles at the lower level pick up the colour of the trees, while the tiles used higher up reflect the blue sky.

The half-timbering, tall chimneys, elaborate porch and deep tiled roof all proclaimed this large detached house to be very much of its time when it was built in 1909.

At the same time as all these innovative styles were becoming accepted and popular, a similar desire for simplicity of design looked back to the classical forms of the Georgian period. This was referred to as the 'Wrenaissance' (after Sir Christopher Wren, who was much admired at that time), and its advocates were known as the neo-Georgians.

As a result of these various influences an eclectic mix of styles emerged which can now be seen as typically Edwardian. Improvements in the standards of design as expressed by both the Arts and Crafts movement and the neo-Georgians were widely espoused and many of their ideas were incorporated into new housing springing up all over Britain. Beams appeared as decorative features and walls were often tile-hung. Elaborate fretwork and wood-turning were used on porches, balconies and gable ends. Pargeting, the old technique of embossing patterns on plasterwork, was revived, and tiles and

This semi-detached house in Letchworth, Hertfordshire, has decorative buttresses at the side, echoing a similar feature found in much grander Arts and Crafts houses of the time.

Decorative windows, whether in coloured glass or with fancy woodwork, as in this semi-detached house, were characteristic of the period.

Folly Farm, Berkshire, dates back to around 1650. Edwin Lutyens was twice commissioned to enlarge it, first in 1906 in seventeenth-century style, and again in 1912, when he designed a new west wing in Arts and Crafts style.

There was quite a vogue for mottoes over front doors and fireplaces. Here the inscription 'ALL GOETH BUT GODDIS WILL' was set above the front door of a superb house. The date and owner's initials are also included.

Right: *Elaborate pargeting was particularly desirable, and here it is set off with a border in classical design. Coloured leaded glass windows and decorative woodwork complete a most attractive exterior.*

Below: *Two examples of the many designs in porches, where the visitor was welcomed to the home.*

This elegant swag of ribbons and flowers is a very attractive example of pargeting on a house of modest size.

windows with Art Nouveau designs became popular.

Classical ideals, too, found favour, particularly in the plainer exteriors of many of the new terraces being built in working-class areas.

When the exterior of the Edwardian house is being considered, the popularity of the balcony cannot be ignored. Following the stuffiness of the Victorian age, fresh air and sunshine now became fashionable, and sleeping in well-aired rooms was much favoured. Sleeping balconies appeared on many larger houses, while on smaller Edwardian villas balconies provided fresh air on summer evenings, as well as being highly decorative.

The restrained simplicity of this detached house, built in 1907, and others of neo-Georgian design, was in stark contrast to the more extravagant designs in vogue at the time.

Built in 1903, this row of terraced houses has a simplicity of design.

Left: *This welcoming cottage-style front door, below a green-leaded glass arch, actually fronts a large terraced house built in 1901 in a smart area of Bristol.*

Below: *A pair of stylish houses with balconies, tall chimneys, pargeting and tile-hanging.*

Above: *The proud occupants pose outside their newly built bungalow in the early 1900s. Despite the apparent lack of a pavement, they have the very latest street light outside their home.*

Even a small villa could display the latest design details. Here the fashionable balcony combines with decorative timbering and embossed terracotta panels. All these features could be produced for the mass market. Decorative terracotta was very fashionable, having been used to great effect by Doultons on the new façade of the Harrods building in Knightsbridge, London.

Left: *With its glass and panelled front door and white-painted balcony, this semi-detached house remains unchanged since it was built in the early years of the twentieth century. The strips of green tiles in the red brickwork are an Arts and Crafts touch unusual on an otherwise ordinary house of the time.*

Above: *The growing number of motor-car owners usually had nowhere to house their vehicles, but motor houses could be purchased. The ones advertised here 'were being sold as fast as they could be made'. Browne & Lilly also advertised stabling, which was generally used before the days of purpose-built garages.*

At the start of the Edwardian period motoring was in its infancy – and indeed, presumed by some to be a short-lived wonder – so no special arrangements were made for accommodating the new-fangled machine. 'Stabling the motor' was the phrase in general use until the 'motor house' became an accepted part of larger homes.

INTERIORS

The general desire to look back to the past for inspiration – with the house a safe haven from the fast-moving changes taking place all around – brought with it a wish to make the interiors of the home more welcoming. Thus a more spacious entrance hall was considered necessary and this led to the creation of the hall living-room, which became extremely fashionable. This was generally included in the new architect-designed houses but in many existing large houses the wall of a room adjacent to the hall needed to be knocked down to produce the extra space required. With the provision of a fireplace and comfortable chairs and sofas, this was a warm and inviting space in which to welcome guests. Here the gentlemen of the house could come indoors in wet clothes and boots, have a warming drink and perhaps smoke a cigarette. As this living-hall was also a general thoroughfare, and by no means private, a man and a woman would be permitted to be there alone together – which would certainly not have been regarded as proper elsewhere in the house.

A cartoon from 'Punch', 1903. The caption under the cartoon reads: 'The latest style of room decoration. The home made beautiful. According to the "Arts & Crafts".' People liked to poke gentle fun at new ideas – note the wide frieze (with its unlikely cats), unusually shaped chairs, decorative 'lily' patterns and 'art' pots.

A delightful gentleman's residence, 'Sunnycroft', Shropshire (now owned by the National Trust), was considerably reconstructed in 1899. At the centre of the house is the fashionable living-hall, which announces the importance of its owners.

This is how 'Everywoman's Encyclopaedia' illustrated an article on the hall sitting-room. 'The fitments are not costly, yet they are in absolute accord with good taste and modern requirements.'

The living-hall was sufficiently popular to be featured in this advertisement by a paint manufacturer.

Newel posts, even in the most modest of Edwardian homes, could be quite elaborate. This one shows Arts and Crafts influence in its angular design.

As always, the latest ideas spread to the houses being built in the new towns and suburbs. Plot sizes were larger than previously available (a new law limited housing to twelve per acre) so there was more space for a hall that was not merely a corridor between rooms. Although in many cases the hall was scarcely large enough to be considered a room, it was now often possible to have the staircase turn at right angles for the last few steps and therefore appear more impressive. Such staircases were often seen in Edwardian houses, together with fancy balusters and newel posts, and in some cases the staircase or other parts of the hall were partially screened to form recesses.

The urge to divide off small areas to give the house a snug feel spread to the

'The Problem for Artistic House Decorators' (1911) includes this picture of a staircase. The author suggests a shaped board to break the line of the landing, and for the pillar, 'if you can find an old Chippendale bedpost – such a pillar will be a really artistic feature.'

Above: *A cosy corner as proposed in 1910. The door has been replaced with an archway and curtain. It is suggested the floor is painted green, with a golden brown rug, the frieze painted white, and the walls panelled and stained an artistic shade of green.*

This is a cosy corner par excellence, incorporating stained glass, ceramic tiles, carved wooden capitals and stonework mosaic. It is at Blackwell, Baillie Scott's Arts and Crafts house in Bowness-on-Windermere, Cumbria.

sitting-room as well. 'Cosy corners' were everywhere at this time, in houses large and small. Sometimes seats facing each other (especially settles) were built in on either side of the fireplace to form a warm alcove. Curtains, too, would be used to form niches, and window seats in casement windows and bays were very popular.

Reception rooms such as the breakfast room, morning room, dining-room, drawing-room, sitting-room or parlour could all be found in an Edwardian house, depending on the social

Charles Rennie Mackintosh's rose-themed drawing-room at The Hill House, Helensburgh (National Trust for Scotland), with its elegant extended window seat. The table is of ebonised wood decorated with tiny mother-of-pearl squares.

standing of its occupants. Upstairs, as well as bedrooms, would be a box room (or lumber room), where trunks, portmanteaux, golf clubs and tennis racquets could be stored. Down below, cellars would be used for storing the large quantities of coal needed in the running of the home, so that scuttles could be replenished without the need to go outside. A coal hole above ground allowed the coalman to deposit the contents of the sacks when he called.

A luxury that had previously been found only in the homes of the upper classes but now became *de rigueur* among the aspiring middle classes was the boudoir. This was a room set aside for the exclusive use of the lady of the house. Here she

Although the brass bed in this bedroom of 1910 has been retained at a time when wooden frames were popular, the rest of the room, with its white-painted furniture and deep frieze, is perfectly of its time.

'A simpler suggestion for a boudoir ... just such a one where so many of the women of England are leading useful, busy, happy lives.' From an item in the 'Lady's Realm'.

could retire to write letters, plan menus, embroider, read or just rest on her chaise-longue to overcome a tiresome headache. To the 'modern woman' – a phrase much used at the time – the boudoir was her equivalent of her husband's study. In many suburban homes the morning room, usually a small room between the kitchen and the other reception rooms, served this purpose although it did not afford the privacy of a boudoir.

Kitchens generally remained small during this period, very much a utilitarian room and not a place where design details were considered important. A scullery off the kitchen was also quite usual, being used for washing clothes and dishes and for other tasks not thought suitable for the kitchen.

This former schoolroom became a smoking-room, then the morning room, at Preston Manor, Brighton, after it was reconstructed in 1905.

The panelled bath shown in this soap advertisement would soon be replaced by a free-standing one.

"Going to the Bath"

Bathrooms, and even indoor lavatories, were becoming more common in all but the poorest homes although they were felt to be merely necessities requiring little space or thought. However, many ladies scorned the use of these dreary bathrooms, much preferring to take a hip bath in front of a warm fire in their bedroom, with their maid providing the hot scented water, as they always had done.

The nursery was still an acknowledged part of the middle- and upper-class home. This was

An Edwardian bedroom bath: a geyser supplies the hot water and the bath tips up to fit into the cupboard.

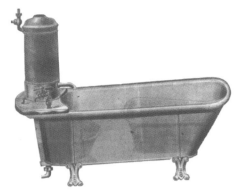

This polished copper geyser, called the 'Cottage Combination', provided hot water and was attached to a tinned-steel bath. It was available from Harrods in 1901 for under £5.

tucked away on an upper floor so that 'King Baby' – as he was commonly referred to in books and magazines of the time – could be looked after by Nurse, far enough away to leave his parents undisturbed.

An important factor in the interior planning of an Edwardian house was the provision that had to be made to accommodate

A nursery designed by Queen Alexandra, the Queen Mother, at the Ideal Home Exhibition and pictured in the 'Illustrated London News', 1913. The design was carried out by Waring & Gillow. The paper confidently advises: 'We can safely say this nursery will be found in many a home'.

These 1901 inner glass front doors are in the most popular colours for home decoration at the time.

staff. Whole floors, reached by the back stairs, were required for the retinues of servants necessary for the efficient running of the large town and country houses. Even in more modest villas small rooms at the top of the house were needed for live-in maids.

Overall, the Edwardian home gave the impression of being far more spacious than its Victorian counterpart. In the main this was due to the more generously sized entrance hall, which set the scene for the rest of the house.

Right and below: *Decorative stained-glass windows were a feature of Arts and Crafts design. These were designed by E. S. Prior (right) and Baillie Scott (below).*

FIXTURES AND FITTINGS

By the beginning of the Edwardian period electricity, which was to bring changes as yet undreamt of in everyday life, was becoming widely used in public buildings. Better-off families soon took advantage of this latest wonder and in newer houses, wherever access to 'the mains' was possible, electricity was installed. However, it was to be many years before it reached the countryside, although owners of large country houses and estates soon purchased one of the 'electric lighting plants' that were advertised in newspapers and magazines.

Meanwhile, gas had reached most homes by the turn of the century and gas mantles provided much of the lighting. Gas burners were surrounded by glass globes, often coloured and frosted to prevent glare, and were either mounted on walls or suspended from a rigid length of gas piping fixed to the ceiling. The little white gas mantles themselves were extremely fragile and a stock of replacements was always kept at hand. The use of gas was supplemented by oil lamps and candles, a candle to light the way to bed being quite usual at this time. For children frightened of the dark, a nightlight – a flat, round candle standing in a saucer of water – provided much reassurance. Not everyone welcomed the bright new electric lighting – women, especially those of more mature years, found it harsh and unflattering after the softer effects of gas and oil lamps.

Central heating, run by solid-fuel boilers, was a luxury available to the few, and open

No Mechanical Knowledge is Required

ASTER Electric Lighting for Country Houses

Above: *An advertisement for lighting for the well-to-do Edwardian home. 'It is so simple and automatic in action that the gardener, the chauffeur, the coachman, or even the handyman can give it the slight attention which is necessary. The light is brilliant, convenient, clean, and very cheaply produced.'*

An electric light fitting from 1906.

These Edwardian light switches and fuse boxes have the name of the Bristol electrician who installed them.

Below: *Some designs for gas fittings from a 1911 article on 'Economy in Lighting': 'some excellent types of gas fittings, artistic in design and practical in application'.*

fires remained as popular as ever. Fireplaces were to be found in most rooms (including the hall and bathrooms in many larger establishments) although heated bedrooms were very much frowned upon at a time when fresh air was much vaunted as essential for good health. Fireplaces and surrounds were much less elaborate than previously. Plainer white-painted Adam-style surrounds were very fashionable, with sometimes a double mantelshelf and maybe a mirror incorporated. The tilework was often of Art Nouveau design, with sinuous flowers and birds, and was generally more delicately

Above: This Edwardian fireplace features a beaten copper hood and green tiles decorated with lilies. It is set in an Adam-style white surround.

The fireplace tiles here are decorated with a delicate sweet-pea design. This flower was said to be Queen Alexandra's favourite and thus enjoyed great popularity at this time.

patterned and coloured than before. For many years people in ordinary homes were distrustful of gas fires and continued to use oil stoves in places where additional heat was needed, such as the hall and landing. Although the burning of oil generated a smell it was regarded as homely and comforting, and the use of such oil stoves continued well into the twentieth century.

Cooking in large established homes was still carried out on vast built-in stoves and in ovens fuelled

Above: *This early-twentieth-century fireplace features not only green tiles in Arts and Crafts style but also an embellished Adam-style surround.*

A fairytale fireplace in the Arts and Crafts style is suggested for the nursery in an article in the 'Lady's Realm'.

by coal. In much smaller houses the kitchen range, again coal-fired, provided the means to cook meals, supply hot water and warm the room. This was very useful in winter but most uncomfortable in summer. The new gas cookers, which could generally be hired from one of the gas companies, made life much easier in middle-class homes, where they were quickly to become popular. They were not only clean and reliable but also allowed the range to be left unlit during warm weather.

Kitchens were merely functional in character, being regarded solely as a workplace and unworthy of further consideration. Large, built-in dressers for the storage of china remained popular, as did built-in larders with tiled shelves and mesh-covered windows to keep food cool, but cabinets that included storage and work surfaces, an idea imported from

The grill in early gas cookers consisted of a small pipe with gas jets, which could be used on top of the stove or turned downwards to grill. The latest addition is shown here – a movable enamelled plate to protect the wall, fitted with a rack for warming plates.

The Gold Medal Eagle Range, a luxury kitchen range, as advertised in a Harrods catalogue early in the twentieth century. This would presumably still need 'black leading' once a week, as did the smaller versions in most homes.

A suggested layout for 'The Ideal Kitchen'. The walls should be in light, bright washable distemper, the floor covered with linoleum, which has a carpet-like design. The table and other surfaces should be covered with pretty imitation tiles of galvanised zinc.

the United States, began to transform kitchens. Perhaps the most noticeable innovation in the Edwardian kitchen was the installation of a sink, previously only to be found in the scullery. Washtubs (known as coppers) were often an integral part of the scullery in the average home. Built of brick and concrete, they housed a metal tub under which a coal fire was lit to heat the water on washdays (usually Monday). In larger houses they would be very large indeed and might be powered by motors run on gas or the new electricity. The washing in such houses would be dried in a large closet in the basement, heated by a central stove.

The Edwardians were very keen on hygiene, so this water filter, advertised as 'germ proof', would have been desirable. The sink is typical of those in most Edwardian kitchens.

In 1906 this was the very latest thing in baths. The metal object at the head of the bath is an elaborate system for unplugging and allowing the water out. The tiles are by William de Morgan, one of the foremost members of the Arts and Crafts movement.

By now, bathrooms were found in many homes though they were usually only just large enough to accommodate the wash-basin, bath and lavatory. Sometimes the lavatory was housed in a separate little room, which was very basic, for although such a facility was necessary the Edwardians preferred not to think about it. Even large houses with many bedrooms would have only one or two bathrooms and lavatories. The outside lavatory remained a feature of most homes. Larger homes had at least two outside lavatories, one or more for the servants and another – frequently hidden discreetly away among the shrubs – for the gentlemen of the

This very grand lavatory has a high-level cistern with a chain. Simpler sanitary ware would be fitted in most homes.

This elaborate shower unit, with shower-heads at various levels, is the sort of bathroom fitting that was available for the very rich.

An advertisement for a Geeko telephone showing 'the old style' and 'the new'. It suggests that a telephone attached to the electric bells (which by now had replaced the old-fashioned bells on springs) would be a time-saving device for servants.

house. Even in better-off homes cut sheets of old newspapers threaded on string hung from a hook next to the lavatory, while in more refined homes boxes containing separate sheets of uncompromisingly shiny lavatory paper might be available.

Few homes had a telephone with outside lines although towards the end of the period they were becoming widespread among the more prosperous addresses. The in-house telephone was popular from the beginning, however. This was wired into most rooms and meant it was far easier to summon a maid than it had been with the old system of bell-pulls and the tube-and-whistle.

Although electricity was later to become almost totally indispensable in the home, in the early years of the twentieth century it was, like so many advanced new inventions, very expensive. It was not until after the First World War, when it had become much cheaper to use, that the wonders of this great new technology would be explored to the full.

Beautifully preserved Art Nouveau decorated brass fingerplates.

A fingerplate designed and made by the Birmingham Guild of Handicrafts. It is of copper and has blue enamel decorations.

FURNISHINGS

It is difficult to be too specific about the furnishings of an average Edwardian house. As the new century dawned people did not just throw out the furniture to which they had grown accustomed. Even young couples setting up home for the first time would have been glad to receive items of old furniture that their relatives could spare. However, the desire to take a fresh look at the home and its furnishings was prevalent at this time, prompted by numerous articles in magazines and newspapers. Illustrations of the latest consumer goods filled their pages, together with suggestions on room settings and advice on colour and style. They extolled the virtues of hygiene in the home, fresh air and sunshine, which were so central to modern thinking. To achieve these ideals, lighter, brighter, less cluttered rooms were called for, and articles under such titles as 'The Noiseless House', 'The Dustproof House' and 'The Sunshine Room' abounded. Ivory-white or a rich soft yellow were suggested for a sunshine room, and around the house clean white paintwork and distempered walls in soft colours or daintily patterned wallpapers were advocated.

This plan for a sunshine room illustrated an article on sunshine and health. 'Sunshine and air mean death to the microbes of our gloomy houses and life to the occupants.' Everything in this room was to be in tints of golden yellow.

In order to make rooms easier to clean, and therefore more hygienic, fewer items of furniture were preferred, with much less ornamentation, so that dust could be kept at bay. Simpler, unpolished furniture, mainly in oak, as favoured by the Arts and Crafts movement, was particularly suited to the current style. Much of the furniture was angular and far less extravagant than previously. Decorative features, hinges, handles and the like were in copper, pewter or black-painted ironwork, rather than the ubiquitous brass of the Victorian years. Display cabinets and bookcases with leaded-glass panels, oak dining tables in a refectory style, and chairs that were rush-seated or in wicker or bamboo all contributed to make the home feel somewhat rustic and cosy. Such furniture was readily available from firms such as Morris & Company, Heal & Son, and Liberty's in Regent Street, London, and gradually, in adapted form, in stores all

Above: *Once again the merits of sunshine are invoked. 'Hall's distemper decoration invites the sunlight – unlike wall paper or paint it never fades or discolours.'*

This original Edwardian fitted dresser is very sturdily made. Contemporary thinking on cleanliness and hygiene would no doubt have required dressers like this to be regularly stripped and washed.

The elegant lines of this chair, with its subtle mother-of-pearl inlay, is typical of those to be found in many Edwardian homes.

over Britain. Liberty's was able to supply not only individual handcrafted items but from 1904 also had its own factory manufacturing furniture and textiles on a significant scale.

For those who favoured eighteenth-century design much well-made reproduction furniture was available. Homes would often contain a mixture of styles, from Sheraton chairs and elegant Regency boudoir suites to Queen Anne sideboards and Jacobean chests, and in 1905 the Chesterfield sofa became especially popular. Delicate inlaid woodwork, and sometimes mother-of-pearl, decorated much of the furniture, which was often quite elegant but rather fragile. Shops such as the newly refurbished Harrods, Selfridges (established in 1909), Waring & Gillow, the Army and Navy

Above: *This advertisement from the 1901 Harrods catalogue shows a dining-room suite (note that a table is not included) in solid walnut, oak or mahogany at £17 5s. In 'second quality' (being from Harrods, it would still no doubt be very well made) it was £15 7s 6d.*

A pipe rack, or smoker's cabinet, would have been very common in Edwardian times, when most men (and some 'fast' women) smoked. This one shows many Arts and Crafts features – it is oak, hand-carved, with copper decorations.

Screens of all kinds – hand-embroidered or home-made with a montage of postcards or scraps – were very useful to form cosy corners or to stand in front of the fireplace.

Stores and many more in London and the provinces could supply everything needed to furnish the modern reproduction home. For some, only the genuine article would do, and antique collecting became a fashionable pastime, which stimulated a proliferation of antique shops.

The very best of both furnishing styles prevailing at the time was costly to produce and therefore expensive to buy. However, the styles were commercially adapted to popular taste, and those living in the growing suburbs and new towns were a

This invoice from Maple & Company, London, dated 1909, includes a mahogany bedstead and bedding, an oak dining table, six oak dining chairs in Morocco and various saucepans. The bill still comes to only £22 16s 2d.

A COTTAGE ROOM

Plain Oak Dresser
No. 505. 4 ft. 6 in. wide
£6 15 0

HEAL
AND
SON

Heal's was one of the first shops to sell craftsman-designed, inexpensive furniture. Furniture such as that advertised here was featured in the Letchworth Exhibition in 1905.

ready market for all the very latest ideas. 'Art' and 'artistic' were words found everywhere in advertisements and features on 'the house beautiful' and were used to describe everything from pottery and metalwork to embroidery and jewellery. Art pottery vases, artistic wrought-iron gates, artistic screens (so useful to create a cosy corner), art pewter jugs and much more were considered part of a tasteful home and showed that the owner was in tune with contemporary thinking.

The fabrics used for upholstery and curtaining reflected both the current styles. Much silk, velvet and brocade, and other expensive materials, were found in the neo-Georgian home, and prettily flowered chintz enjoyed a surge of popularity as it fitted in well with the

A girl's rose bedroom, in which 'Comfort is combined with daintiness'. The large hat box, curtained shelves for boots and linoleum flooring are all used as selling points.

An art pottery vase, especially from Doulton's (as here) or one of the other high-quality potteries, would be a much-prized possession and accordingly displayed in a prominent position in the home.

Right: *This corner fitment with its sofa seat, bookcase, cupboard and china shelf cost £30 and provided a ready-made cosy corner in the latest style.*

desired lighter décor. However, less opulent fabrics such as cotton and wool, in plain colours or simpler designs, were admired elsewhere and any that were hand-woven, or even gave the impression of being so, were very much in vogue. Likewise, floor coverings mirrored the rest of the furnishings: thick carpets, often with elaborate traditional patterns, complemented the classical home, while

This breakfast table setting is shown in an article under the heading 'A well-arranged table dispels frowns'. It advises: 'Porridge, and cereal foods should be very daintily served, or they are apt to look messy.'

A 1903 'Old Studio' sideboard by Liberty's, displaying items perhaps of the Celtic-inspired Cymric silver and Tudric pewter, which were available at that time.

Below: *In this layout for a drawing-room the frieze is to be finished with black beading and the mantelpiece painted black. Likewise, all woodwork should be black, and the floor covered with Indian matting, on which are laid rose-coloured rugs.*

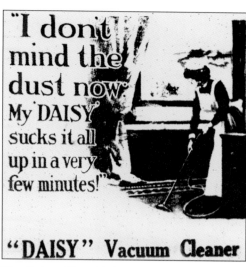

The Daisy (Electric) Vacuum Cleaner could be purchased for 15 guineas. The advertisement mentions cars racing past at what would have seemed high speed, sending dust into the house through the open windows.

Vacuum-cleaner nozzles such as this, into which a tube arrangement could be inserted, led down to a huge suction pump in the basement of large Edwardian houses.

The caption under this 'Punch' cartoon from September 1908 reads: 'Thank goodness, there you are, Augustus. For heaven's sake take the children away, and er, is there any supper for them, or I shall never get this done in time for the Ideal Home Exhibition.' Meanwhile the mother's artistic creation bears the words 'Ye hande that rockes ye cradle'.

No Edwardian home should be without a fern on a stand: 'To have a pot of ferns, or the ever-useful palm … is beginning to be considered essential … The effect of plants placed at a height is so good that the pot stand is much in demand.'

wood-block flooring, stained and waxed floorboards or linoleum scattered with rush matting, hand-made rugs or copies of oriental rugs were the choice in the 'artistic' home.

Carpets had previously been swept with a broom, and rugs shaken outside, but the new patent carpet-sweeper, lightweight and hand-powered, was now available. In 1901 the vacuum-cleaner was patented by Hubert Cecil Booth, an Englishman. A long tube led from the machine, which was fitted in a horse-drawn cart, and inserted through the doors or windows of a building to suck out the dirt. The electrically operated vacuum-cleaner soon followed. This could be handled by a single servant and was easy to use; it was generally plugged in the electric light fitting in the absence of electrical sockets.

It has to be said that, in spite of widely promulgated opinion advocating less clutter and more style about the home, the average Edwardian room would still appear to modern eyes overfurnished and somewhat fussy. As with every generation, much-loved family pieces – furniture and ornaments – would share space with the latest novelties, and it was in the newer homes that the changes were most noticeable. Perhaps the only piece of furniture, other than necessary household items, which was found in homes both great and small was a tall plant stand. Either polished and elegant, or more angular and light-coloured, this universally loved possession, instead of the old-fashioned aspidistra, now carried an elegant fern.

THE GARDEN

The Edwardian garden differed greatly from that of the previous century. Gone were the serried rows of annuals, neat borders and Victorian shrubberies. Instead, two completely different garden styles emerged to match the houses they surrounded.

The formal garden style of the eighteenth century was considered desirable to complement the elegant, classically inspired houses. They required plenty of space to set off the wide vistas and follies. In particular there was a revival of the parterre, an ornamental arrangement of flower beds with little paths, adorned with statues and urns. From the past, too, came a renewed interest in topiary, as well as knot gardens and herb gardens, all of which were taken up with much enthusiasm for historical accuracy.

However, the ethos of the Arts and Crafts movement encompassed the garden as well as the house, and it was Gertrude Jekyll above all who successfully incorporated these ideals into her gardens. Working on commissions with the architect Edwin Lutyens, she designed gardens with riotous borders of hardy plants whose myriad colours seemed to merge naturally but were in fact the product of her trained

A fragment of artistic colour set in a garden wall. The tilework is by William de Morgan.

This delightful picture
by Elizabeth Earnshaw,
entitled 'My Lady's
Garden', comes from
'The Girl's Own
Annual' of 1909 and is
an idealised version of
the perfect Edwardian
garden. Fitting so well
with the colour scheme
prevalent at the time, the
peacock with its plumage
of blue and green
appeared in all manner
of Arts and Crafts items.

The title of this 'Punch' cartoon from 1913 is 'The Home Beautiful – the opening of the rockery season in our garden suburb'.

artist's eye and detailed planning. The use of vernacular materials, in keeping with the house, gave rise to paths and walls in rough-hewn stone or mellow brickwork. Long shady pergolas, rose-covered archways and pathways whose edges were strewn with a colourful profusion of perennials graced these gardens.

Miss Jekyll designed for the rich but her ideas spread quickly and were perfectly in tune with the times. Those with new homes in the suburbs and garden cities, and elsewhere, had space of their

A late-summer herbaceous border in Hestercombe Gardens, Somerset. These gardens were originally by Gertrude Jekyll, working together with the architect Edwin Lutyens, and have been magnificently restored.

Part of the restored Jekyll garden near the orangery at Hestercombe, as seen through the grille of the gate in the wall designed by Lutyens. Grey foliage and lavender sprawl over the paving in a delightfully natural way.

own to cultivate. Cottage-style 'natural' gardens became extremely popular, with roses, honeysuckle, hollyhocks, lupins, delphiniums and many other 'old-world' flowers tumbling over trellises and archways, or edging a little courtyard. Features such as urns, sundials, garden seats and rustic shelters could be readily purchased. Furniture especially made for the garden was something new for all but the rich. For most people it had been quite usual to move a small table and chairs from indoors in order to enjoy the sunshine. Now all

This picture illustrates an article on 'Meals out of doors', before garden furniture became more widely available. The table is set just as it would be indoors, and there is even a side table available in the form of the so-called butler's tray.

In this photograph, taken early in the twentieth century, the family are sitting on their veranda, taking advantage of the fresh air – even though it is obvious that the front lawn could do with being mown!

manner of canework and wicker furniture was available, which soon appeared in many gardens, allowing ordinary folk in towns and suburbs to enjoy their leisure hours in cottage garden surroundings.

The Dryad Cane Works produced this garden furniture. According to the caption, 'cane furniture is made in all manner of quaint and picturesque shapes ... Nothing could be more pleasing to the artistic sense than a few cane chairs grouped on a grassy lawn.'

In pursuit of the cult of fresh air, a conservatory could be adapted to form an ideal breakfast-house, the glass roof being retained and the sides left open, as shown here.

The garden became, for the first time, an extension of the house, and this was particularly the case for those following the 'fresh air for good health' principle. Articles praising the benefits of outdoor sleeping were illustrated with examples of various wooden sheds manufactured for this purpose. These would have wooden walls on three sides only, plus a roof for cover. Some could revolve freely, keeping the occupant shielded from the wind. Somewhat surprisingly, these open-air bedrooms were thought equally beneficial for babies and small children, who apparently needed to be gradually weather-hardened so that 'by the time the cold weather comes he will have become thoroughly accustomed to it'.

This garden-bedroom is one of many designs available for sleeping out of doors. During the long summer days it could be adapted as an open-air sitting-room.

A PERIOD OF CHANGE

For the Edwardians, great changes were taking place all around. 'Whatever will they be up to next?' summed up the feelings of most people towards this bewildering progress. But life in the home was becoming far more pleasant, with new ways to spend the increasing leisure hours. The piano had become more commonplace, although it was still something of a status symbol. A choice of colour and style – painted, reproduction Chippendale, emulating an Elizabethan virginal, or in the latest 'artistic' taste – meant that pianos could be bought to suit any room.

Moreover, new technology was creeping into the home. The gramophone, invented in 1895, came into its own during this period. These early machines were wound up by hand and sound was transferred from a disc through a large horn. Most were so loud that it was recommended that they be played in another room or in the garden, where 'the beauty of the record

An advertisement for a piano from the 'Lady's World Magazine', 1901. With an Italian walnut case and gilt sconces, this piano cost 20 guineas and would have taken pride of place in the home at the time. Also advertised are organs priced from 8 guineas, harmoniums from 6 guineas, a midget organette at 13 shillings, and concertinas and accordions from 3 shillings and 6 pence, providing home-made music for the leisure hours.

PHONOGRAPHS!   GRAPHOPHONES!
GRAMAPHONES!   TALKING MACHINES!

Best house in the trade for Machines, Sundries
and Records of all Makes. Prompt delivery.

No Cheap Rubbish, but Every Machine Guaranteed Perfect.

EASY TERMS ARRANGED.

WE are the largest dealers in this line and have machines at all
prices from **10/6.** Our record stock exceeds **100,000**
Cylinder and Disc Records of all makes, so we can promptly execute
orders to customers' own selections. Write for our Catalogue and you
will be surprised at our prices.

Repairs.   Machines on Hire.   Machines Exchanged.
RECORDS EXCHANGED.

SPECIAL OFFERS FOR CASH.   PACKED FREE ON RAIL.

No. 1 "Dulcetto" Phono, a perfect reproducing machine,
complete with six assorted records, latest band selections,
comic songs and recitations 18/6

No. 3 "Dulcetto," complete in handsome cabinet fitted with
recorder with which own records can be made. Six
assorted records and six blanks. Wonderful value 45/6

Dulcetto Special Phono, a highest grade instrument fitted in
splendid cabinet complete with special recording apparatus,
good horn, etc., 12 assorted records and 6 blanks. A
first-class outfit 80/-

Write at once for Catalogue (post free)
or call.

THE PHONO EXCHANGE, 44, BERNERS STREET, OXFORD
STREET, LONDON, W.

Hours 9 to 8.   Wholesale and retail.

This advertisement, from a 1902 copy of the 'London Magazine', mentions not only the gramophone (but spelt with an 'a' in the middle syllable) but also phonographs, graphophones and talking machines. The advertiser's stock exceeded 100,000 cylinder and disc records.

will be heard with considerably less volume, and all surface
noise eliminated', as a contemporary advertisement advised.
Edwardians were thrilled, however, to hear for the first time
whole orchestras, famous singers and even the new ragtime
music in their own homes. Those with a telephone could, for £5
per year, subscribe to the Electrophone. This, with the help of
an induction coil, batteries and two receivers, made it possible
to listen in directly to West End shows or even a sermon from
St Martin-in-the-Fields church in London.

Progress in what we would now term labour-saving devices
was slow. Servants had always been readily available, and
cheap to employ, so there had been no need for such
improvements. However, with more openings for women to
work in the growing number of shops, new telephone
exchanges or expanding offices and factories, the 'servant
problem' became a worrying concern in many
homes. In this climate it was not long before
several early machines were invented to help
lighten the housewife's load. Electricity made
possible the first electric irons, vacuum-
cleaners, fires, kettles and washing machines,
though it was not for some years that ways
were found to combine the use of electricity
with water, so heating elements were strapped

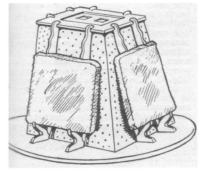

Illustrating an article from 1911 on 'Gas-stove improvements', this strange machine is captioned 'A contrivance by which four pieces of bread may be toasted at one time on a gas-ring in two minutes'.

This Turkish bath appears to be a sort of waterproof box with an opening for the head. A chair is placed inside, together with a spirit stove on which water can be heated to provide the necessary steam.

Below: This 'quick-boiling' kettle (1911), sitting on a single gas ring, had a metal jacket that confined the heat around the sides of the kettle. This was said not only to cause the kettle to boil faster but to save gas consumption by one third.

Below: Such items as these, for home embroidery, were featured in many magazines. Women were keen to enhance their home with items fashioned in their spare time.

outside. For ladies, electric curling tongs and even the first rather basic hair-dryers were now available, and, in the garden, the first motor lawnmowers arrived in 1905.

Except for the poor, for whom life remained a struggle, these were good years for the average Edwardian. After a long day at work, a warm and welcoming house awaited along a gas-lit street and home comforts were more plentiful than ever before. With the exception of the war years, this pattern of life, incorporating more and more home improvements and increased leisure time, was to continue through the whole of the twentieth century. The house style that was created in the Edwardian period has had a lasting effect on domestic architecture in Britain and can still be seen in many of the homes in suburban streets and estates today. Perhaps the nostalgia felt in those days for a time when life seemed more simple and contented still strikes a chord with us today.

FURTHER READING

Anscombe, Isabelle, and Gere, Charlotte. *Arts and Crafts in Britain and America*. Academy Editions, 1978.

Aslet, Clive. *The Last Country Houses*. Yale University Press, 1982.

Barker, Michael. *Sir Edwin Lutyens*. Shire, 2005.

Bloom, Ursula. *Sixty Years of Home*. Hurst & Blackett, 1960.

Brown, Jane. *Gardens of a Golden Afternoon*. Penguin, new edition 1994 (originally published by Allen Lane, 1982).

Cumming, Elizabeth, and Kaplan, Wendy. *The Arts and Crafts Movement*. Thames & Hudson, 1991.

Davey, Peter. *Arts and Crafts Architecture*. Phaidon, 1995.

Hackney, Fiona and Isla. *Charles Rennie Mackintosh*. Grange Books, 1989.

Haigh, Diane. *Baillie Scott: The Artistic House*. Academy Editions, 1995.

Hitchmough, Wendy. *The Arts and Crafts Home*. Pavilion, 2000.

Hockman, Hilary. *Edwardian House Style*. David & Charles, 1994.

Massingham, Betty. *Gertrude Jekyll*. Shire, 1975; reprinted 2000.

Morris, Barbara. *Liberty Design 1874–1914*. Pyramid, 1989.

Pearsall, Ronald. *Edwardian Life and Leisure*. David & Charles, 1973.

Priestley, J. B. *The Edwardians*. Sphere Books, 1970.

The heated towel rail was one of the inventions of the Edwardian period. Before that, towels had been warmed in front of the bedroom fire when baths had been taken there.

The 'home healthy', an Edwardian obsession, was even referred to in an advertisement for Fry's cocoa. This is pictured on the back page of 'Mother and Home', 1910.

Places to Visit

Blackwell, Bowness-on-Windermere, Cumbria LA23 3JT. Telephone: 01539 446139. Website: www.blackwell.org.uk

Castle Drogo, Drewsteignton, Exeter, Devon EX6 6PB (National Trust). Telephone: 01647 433306. Website: www.nationaltrust.org.uk

Cheltenham Art Gallery, Clarence Street, Cheltenham, Gloucestershire GL50 3JT. Telephone: 01242 237431. Website: www.cheltenhammuseum.org.uk

The Debenham House, 8 Addison Road, London W14 8DJ. Telephone: 07989 967147. Website: www.debenhamhouse.com This is a private house but a very good view of the exterior can be seen from the pavement in Addison Road.

First Garden City Heritage Museum, 296 Norton Way South, Letchworth Garden City, Hertfordshire SG6 1SU. Telephone: 01462 482710. Website: www.gardencitymuseum.org

The Geffrye Museum, Kingsland Road, London E2 8EA. Telephone: 020 7739 9893. Website: www.geffrye-museum.org.uk

Hestercombe Gardens, Cheddon Fitzpaine, Taunton, Somerset TA2 8LG. Telephone: 01823 413923. Website: www.hestercombe.com

The Hill House, Upper Colquhoun Street, Helensburgh, Scotland G84 9AJ. Telephone: 08444 932208. Website: www.nts.org.uk

Museum of Domestic Design and Architecture, Middlesex University, Cat Hill, Barnet, Hertfordshire EN4 8HT. Telephone: 020 8411 5244. Website: www.moda.mdx.ac.uk

Preston Manor, Preston Drove, Brighton, East Sussex BN1 6SD. Telephone: 01273 290900. Website: www.prestonmanor.virtualmuseum.info

Standen, West Hoathly Road, East Grinstead, West Sussex RH19 4NE (National Trust). Website: www.nationaltrust.org.uk

Sunnycroft, 200 Holyhead Road, Wellington, Telford, Shropshire TF1 2DR (National Trust). Telephone: 01952 242884. Website: www.nationaltrust.org.uk

Victoria and Albert Museum, Cromwell Road, South Kensington, London SW7 2RL. Telephone: 020 7942 2000. Website: www.vam.ac.uk

OUR GARDEN SUBURB—ITS BRIGHT SIDE.

The genteel aspirations of the middle classes are satirised in this 'Punch' cartoon from 1913, entitled 'Our Garden Suburb – Its Bright Side'. The text beneath reads: 'Mr & Mrs Hogarth-Jenkins, 89 Ruskin Close and Mr & Mrs Derwent-Potts, 90 Ruskin Close. AT HOME July 3rd 2.30–6. LAWN TENNIS. RSVP to either address.'

INDEX